ENGLISH TEATIME TREATS

DELICIOUS TRADITIONAL RECIPES MADE SIMPLE

SANDRA HAWKINS

Copyright © 2016 Sandra Hawkins

All rights reserved. No part of this publication may be reproduced, distributed, or transmitted in any form or by any means, including photocopying, recording, or other electronic or mechanical methods, without the prior written permission of the publisher, except in the case of brief quotations embodied in reviews and certain other noncommercial uses permitted by copyright law.

Published by Great British Book Publishing, London

ISBN: 978-0-9957623-0-5
ISBN: 978-0-9957623-1-2

DEDICATION

To my amazing husband, Simon, and our children,
Poppy, Monty and Barty.

TABLE OF CONTENTS

Introduction	01
Tea	09
Scones	19
Cakes	35
Round	37
Square	51
Loaf and Rock	65
Biscuits	83
Snappy	87
Shortbreads	97
Exotic English Teatime Treats	115
Old English Pikelets	153
Savories	159
Finger Sandwiches	161
Mini Yorkshire Puddings	169
Putting It All Together: An English Afternoon Tea Celebration	175

INVITATION

You are cordially invited to become an English Teatime Treater!

Sign up at the website below and you will receive a FREE video demonstration of one of the recipes from this book! Check out the website for up-to-date promotions, competitions, the release dates of future books, and all the latest news!

WWW.ENGLISHTEATIMETREATS.COM

INTRODUCTION

"I would love to make an English Teatime Treat recipe, but it would take ages and I just don't have the time!"

"I don't really know where to start in baking something from scratch, as I've heard it's really complicated to bake and you have to be so precise with the quantities."

"I just can't face getting out my electric mixer, assuming I can find the right attachments for it, and I hate all the cleaning up!"

Do any of these thoughts sound familiar? If so, you're not alone!

However, don't despair! The English Teatime Treat recipes in this book are quick, easy and need very little cleaning up afterward!

Not many people have very much time to spend in the kitchen, so most recipes are less than 30 minutes from measure to munch. What I mean by that is that you can begin the recipe and in under 30 minutes, you can be eating your creations!

That means you could walk into your kitchen, choose your recipe, measure out the ingredients and be munching a chocolate shortbread within 30 minutes and most of those 30 minutes will be waiting for the shortbread to cook or cool down enough to munch!

To make one of these recipes, all you need to do is scoop out the ingredients and follow the simple instructions. I have set out the quantities in easy-to-measure amounts. It really is that straightforward.

I guarantee:

- No electric mixers or food gadgets
- No rubbing in and no rolling out
- No pile of cleaning up, and
- You don't need any special training or experience to make any of these recipes.

You need just a saucepan, your cup measures and a pan for the oven.

Picture the scene. You get a call from your friend you haven't seen for a while who wants to drop by in 30 minutes. Your house needs some attention (if you're anything like me) and you don't have much in the way of refreshments to offer her. What do you do to make your friend feel welcome?

Choose one of the 30 minutes from measure to munch recipes, for example, ginger snap biscuits and you're good to go.

Measure out and mix, pop the biscuits into the oven, then use the cooking time to have a quick tidy up. The biscuits come out the oven and onto the cooling rack. The doorbell goes and your friend walks into a home and is greeted with the smell of freshly baked ginger snaps, all ready for a good catch-up. Plus, of course, the question, "Where did you get these biscuits?" To which you reply, "Oh, I made them from scratch!"

Of course, I'm being flippant. Your friend has come to see you and catch-up, not to be impressed by your baking. But you have turned a simple catch-up into an occasion.

Perhaps someone is going through a difficult time and you want to let him or her know that you are thinking about them. Or perhaps they've had some good news and you want to do something special to celebrate.

I have learned that people are truly touched when you make something for them, and treat them as worthy of your effort and time, even though only you know how very quick and easy it was to do!

These recipes can help you to turn a catch-up into an occasion, an achievement into a celebration and to bring back the wonderful homey fragrance of baking for someone you care about. I hope this book will help you to seize life's delights and transform them into moments.

I have included a copious number of fun facts with the recipes, so that you can have a bit of fun with your friends, and not only enjoy the delicious baking, but also a little light-hearted chat.

For example, did you know that Her Majesty Queen Elizabeth II actually made Dropped Scones for President Dwight Eisenhower when he visited Balmoral Castle in 1959, that it was in America that tea bags were invented and that the Victoria Sandwich Cake was actually created for Queen Victoria?

I live in a little English village by the seaside and have been taught to cook by my mother, grandmothers, great aunts and my Food and Nutrition teacher, Mrs Potts (yes - her real name!). I have been cooking teatime treats since childhood. Testing and searching through countless traditional English recipes, I have reinvented, re-adjusted and refined them so that each one is an absolute treat and easy to prepare.

Having studied Chemistry in college, I have carefully researched the amazing processes that transform simple ingredients into mouth-watering treats. I have re-engineered complicated recipes to be really easy to prepare.

I want to bring back the joy of cooking and eating simple yet delicious teatime treats. So much cookery has become overly fancy, mixing flavors and textures in a way that is too complicated to enjoy. Food does not need to be fancy to be fantastic.

I have maintained the profound alchemy of simple wholesome ingredients mixed together to produce something amazing. Not pointlessly fancy, but wholesomely good.

It always amazes me how simple ingredients are transformed by the process of baking into something which is so much more than their individual parts. True alchemy happens in the kitchen.

Let me take you on an adventure in cooking delicious teatime treats. You will know exactly what is in everything you, your children, friends and family are eating - no nasty surprises. It will be easy and taste absolutely delicious - from measure to munch in no time, with no messy pile of cooking utensils to clean afterward.

How special will your friends feel, thinking that you must have toiled for ages over that cake made from scratch! They won't know how easy it is, unless you tell them!

I guarantee that if you prepare a few of these recipes, you will never want to buy or eat a factory made treat again! New family eating traditions will be created to enhance your home.

Having experienced Afternoon Tea at Fortnum & Mason's in the Diamond Jubilee Tea Salon in London, opened by Her Majesty Queen Elizabeth II in 2012, and Barristers Chambers' Tea in Lincoln's Inn, London, I would love to introduce you to these delicious recipes from England.

Start today by making something from one of the chapters. What about shortbread infused with lavender - the delight of the Elizabethan Court in the 1600s, or chocolate Tiffin inspired from the days of the English Raj or Medieval Honey Cake using spices from the Crusades!

The recipes in this book are split into six parts:

1. Scones
2. Cakes, round, square, loaf and rock
3. Biscuits, snappy and shortbreads
4. Exotic English Teatime Treats
5. Old English Pikelets
6. Savories

While this book sets out teatime recipes, I have included a final section showing how you can serve up these treats in a traditional English way, as an English Afternoon Tea Celebration.

In the recipes, I have used US cup measures because using these make the recipes so easy. For my European friends, I would encourage you to buy some. They are available very cheaply on the internet. At the back of the book, I have added a handy conversion table for butter and oven temperatures.

Before I introduce the recipes, I cannot continue without a little word about the drink that gives teatime its name. I'm talking about the beverage, hot tea. I'll introduce some fun facts about how teatime actually came to be a thing, surprisingly how an American has influenced the way the English drink tea and how to make your best cup of tea ever!

THE IDEA OF TEA

Where did the idea of drinking tea come from? We must look back into antiquity to ancient China.

Legend has it that in 2737 B.C. the emperor of China, Shen Nung, discovered tea by accident. He was resting under a wild tea bush, boiling some water, and some leaves from the bush fluttered down. They fell into his water. He drank it, liked the taste and the rest is history!

In England, many years later, it was the Portuguese Princess, Catherine of Braganza, who really made tea-drinking popular. She brought tea with her to England as part of her dowry when she married Charles II in 1662. Now, you can imagine the Princess as the Kate Middleton of her day. Everyone was fascinated by how Catherine lived and wanted to emulate her.

Drinking tea became a passion of the aristocracy. Men drank tea in coffee houses and women had tea parties at home. Even the famous diarist Samuel Pepys wrote on June 28, 1667, "Home, and there find my wife making of tea".

There is a wonderful hidden gem of a store in London's The Strand. It is Twining's Tea Store. I say hidden because it has a very narrow front and is easily missed. From these premises, tea has been sold for over 300 years! What is interesting are the old artifacts associated with tea in cases along the walls.

 In 1784, tea could finally be drunk by the general population when the British Government lifted the heavy tax on tea. At last, it was affordable for all.

Tea became so important for morale that the British Government took over the tea trade during the World Wars so that its supply would be guaranteed.

But it actually took an American, Thomas Sullivan, to make the process of drinking tea far less messy and far easier! Thomas successfully marketed a small, porous bag that contains tea leaves and shipped them around the world in about 1904. Now, in 2016, most tea is drunk using tea bags.

REFRAMING THE BOSTON TEA PARTY INCIDENT

It is a great shame that tea itself has received such a bad name after being hurled into the sea during the Boston Tea Party. Of course, as you know, it wasn't actually the tea that was the problem, but the tax. In fact, the Governor of Boston as well as most of the population of Boston enjoyed drinking tea!

Being unfairly taxed without representation was the heart of the matter. Perhaps the Boston Tea Party should be renamed, the "No Taxation without Representation Party" (Although, that's not quite as catchy!) and tea should be set free from the shackles of that association!

In any event, tea is a wonderfully refreshing beverage which has health benefits recognized for millennia. It is also a good excuse to eat some of these delicious teatime treats!

WHEN IS TEATIME?

You know the sinking feeling around 4 o'clock? After lunch, but too early for dinner? Well, in the early 1800s, the Duchess of Bedford, Anna Maria Stanhope, one of Queen Victoria's ladies-in-waiting, suffered from exactly that 'sinking feeling' at about 4 o'clock every day.

At first, the Duchess asked her servants to sneak her a pot of tea and a few baked treats. But as she so enjoyed this, she began inviting friends to join her in her rooms at Belvoir Castle. Rather like a midnight feast in the afternoon! Teatime was born.

Having participated in various teatime ceremonies, including the rituals of a Japanese Tea Ceremony in Tokyo, teatime with three village chiefs in Nigeria, and English Afternoon Tea at Fortnum and Mason's in Piccadilly, London, tea has its own etiquette! But the most important aspects will always remain the tea and the treats and the enjoyment!

In fact, when I was a pupil barrister (or law student as you would call it in the United States), in a Barrister's Chambers at London's Lincoln's Inn, everything stopped for tea. The courts ended at 4 o'clock enabling the Barristers to return to their Chambers for tea. We used to meet at 4:15 pm, sharp, in the Head of Chambers room where the Clerks would deliver a very large pot of tea - always half Earl Grey and half English Breakfast Tea - with cold milk and biscuits. Standing around the table with the teapot, we would hear how the day's activities in court had progressed.

The quality and type of biscuit were of the utmost importance to these Chambers Tea discussions. Actually, I distinctly remember that a senior member of Chambers telephoned down to the Clerks and complained bitterly and volubly about the lack of interesting biscuits available - I don't think he had had a very good day in Court!

I shall let Bilbo Baggins have the last word. He says to his fellow adventurers at the end of *The Hobbit*, "Tea is at four; but any of you are welcome at any time!"

WHICH BRAND OF TEA IS BEST?

I am talking only about black tea, which does not include the many different flavored teas that you can buy. Lipton, Bigalow and Twining are the top three best-selling black teas in the U.S. All I really want to say about which is the best, is that **you** should find the tea that you like the most. It is worth trying a few to discover which one suits your palate. I recently blind-tasted a variety of branded and supermarket teas to discover that the one I had been drinking was still my favorite!

Some people can be rather superior and talk about single varieties of tea and tea from particular plantations etc., but leaving all that aside, what matters is your own personal taste. I like to drink English Breakfast Tea, which is strong, with cold milk in the morning and at teatime, and usually I drink Earl Grey tea, which has a hint of bergamot in it, without milk, at other times of the day.

LEAF TEA OR TEA BAGS?

Though first marketed and exported from America, the tea bag really took off in the 1970s in Britain. It means that there is no mess to clean up after enjoying your cup of tea. As you can imagine there is some snobbishness about using the leaf rather than bags, but why make a mess you have to clean up? I say, go for the bag and have a great cuppa!

HEALTH BENEFITS

The health benefits of tea have been thoroughly researched. Many studies claim that it may reduce the risk of heart attacks and help avoid various forms of cancer due to the presence of antioxidants in tea. Tea is also linked to lowering your risk of Parkinson's disease. So boil up some water and brew a cup!

HOW TO MAKE TEA

Please don't feel insulted to find a section on how to make tea. The thing is, I have ordered tea in many different parts of the globe and more often than not, it is desperately disappointing! Apart from having a reasonably good tea bag, there is one essential secret to tea-making. I shall share it with you. Ready? The water must be almost boiling. That's it!

If almost boiling water is used, the tea will be great. My heart sinks when a warm glass of water arrives with a tea bag on the side because I know the tea cannot be salvaged. If only the bag could be popped in when very hot water is poured into the cup or mug, all would be well.

If you think you don't like hot tea, I challenge you to try making it as I've set out below. Be prepared to change your mind!

I would recommend using a tea bag and a mug for daily use, and a teapot and cups for a more formal Afternoon Tea. It should be easy, and it is easy!

Let me take you through the steps to create your best cup of tea ever, with a tea bag in a mug:

1. Fill your stove-top kettle with fresh water, you need lots of oxygen in the water to help with the brewing process, (I was taught by Mrs. Potts that the water should be freshly drawn - but that sounds as though it's coming from a well!) and turn it on.

2. Put a tea bag in your mug while the kettle is boiling, and get out the cold milk.

3. Once the kettle has boiled, pour water over the tea bag and fill up your mug to within about 1 inch from the top.

4. Leave to brew for 3-5 minutes.

5. Use a teaspoon to fish out the bag and add a little cold milk - I would suggest about a ½ inch.

6. If you like sugar, now is the time to add it.

7. Drink while hot and enjoy.

Now, the steps to create your best tea ever, using a teapot and cups:

1. Fill your stove-top kettle with fresh water and turn it on.

2. Assemble the pot, cups, the creamer for the milk (make sure it's cold), sugar and teaspoons, while the kettle is boiling.

3. Once the kettle has boiled, warm the teapot by pouring in a little of the boiling water and swirling it around your pot. Pour out that water.

4. Add either your loose leaf tea, one teaspoon per person and one for the pot, or add the number of bags required (one per person).

5. Fill the pot with your almost boiling water. Give it a stir for a few seconds with a teaspoon.

6. Put the lid on the pot, and the tea cozy (mine was knitted by my mom). If you don't have a tea cozy, wrap up the pot with a couple of tea towels and leave to brew for 3-5 minutes.

7. When ready to pour, if you used loose leaf tea, place your tea strainer over the cup or mug, pour out the hot tea first and then add the milk. Add sugar as necessary.

8. Drink while hot.

CONCLUDING REMARKS

Now you know a little about tea, how teatime was created and how to enjoy a refreshing cup of tea. What's needed now are some delicious treats to eat with your tea! I shall start our journey into English teatime treats with scones. These are so easy to prepare and whenever you are presented with Afternoon Tea in England, scones, preserves and cream are always essential.

These delicious mounds can be either served warm or cold but always with preserves and cream. I have kept my promise, no electric mixers, not even rubbing in or rolling out is required.

SCONES

INTRODUCTION

Remember my guarantee, no electric mixers or food gadgets, no rubbing in and no rolling out? Here I have re-adjusted the traditional scone recipe so that you don't have any rubbing in of the fat into the flour. But this recipe still gives you wonderful scones!

What is a scone? Well, it's a little bit like an American biscuit, but more crumbly and is usually served with preserves and cream.

Traditionally, the scone is split in half and spread with strawberry jam and a generous blob of clotted or scalded cream. However, you obviously should add the preserve of your choice or even jelly (I'm not sure how well grape jelly would work, but if that's your thing, go for it!) and then top it off with cream.

In fact, there is a long-standing dispute between the counties of Devon and Cornwall in England as to the correct order of applying the preserves and cream to your scone. Those from Devon, favor cream first then preserves. Those from Cornwall favor preserves first then cream.

We have always added preserves followed by cream in our family! I have tried it both ways and have found that the preserve seems to meld better with the scone if applied first. But try it both ways and you decide whether the Devon or Cornish method is best!

Now to the cream. Clotted cream may sound odd but it is a special kind of cream from the West Country in England, Devon or Cornwall, and is thicker because it has had its whey removed. It is delicious, but it is an acquired taste, not to mention quite difficult to find in America.

I'm all for taking inspiration from traditions and making them work for today. In order to have an English experience, I suggest that you either whip up some cream, or use some aerosol whipped cream to finish off the scones. Aerosol cream doesn't hold its shape for that long, so don't leave them too long before eating.

These scones are very evocative of summer afternoon cream teas in English scented gardens. They are easy, light, simple scones for your afternoon tea - but what delicious show-stoppers!

Scones themselves are so much better if handled very little. In each of these recipes, it should be your goal to touch the mixture as little as possible.

RICH SCONES

30 Min

FUN FACT

The first recorded use of the word scone was in the early 1500s. How should it be pronounced? It either rhymes with gone or tone. Both are acceptable, but my family always pronounces it rhyming with gone.

INGREDIENTS (MAKES 10-12)

¼ cup (or ½ stick) butter

¼ cup milk

¼ cup water

2 cups of self-rising flour, extra for the scone stamping-out stage

1 teaspoon baking soda

1 tablespoon superfine sugar

1 egg

Cookie sheet, a round pastry cutter 2 ¼ inches, failing that a glass turned upside down dusted with flour.

METHOD

1. Pre-heat the oven to 400° F.

2. Put the butter in a 3- or 4-quart saucepan and warm it until it is almost melted. You want it to be almost completely melted, but as cool as possible. It is the melted butter which adds such a lovely flavor to the scones.

3. Add to your saucepan of melted butter the milk and water.

4. Tip in the flour, baking soda and sugar on top of the butter mixture.

5. Make a well in the flour mixture and add the egg into the well.

6. Mix everything together lightly until all the liquid is incorporated into the flour. It will be very soft and that's fine.

7. Sprinkle your work surface with some flour and tip out your scone dough. It will need a little gathering together but if it is too sticky to handle, add a little more flour.

8. No rolling, just pat the dough to a depth of about 1 inch and stamp out your scones using a cookie cutter or glass dusted with flour. Place them on your cookie sheet - no need to grease the sheet.

9. Gather together the leftover dough and repeat the stamping out until all the dough is used.

10. Pop the scones into the oven for about 10-12 minutes.

11. These delicious scones should have risen beautifully and will be slightly golden on the top. Remove and place on a cooling rack.

12. Leave to cool - or just try one split in half with butter!

When cool or cold, split in half, spread with the preserve of your choice and top them off with a blob or squirt of cream. They are little mouthfuls of heaven!

WONDERFUL VARIATIONS

FRUITED SCONES

Raisins, Golden Raisins, Glacé Cherries

FUN FACT

Raisins were brought back from the Crusades and used in cooking. The famous English Plum Pudding was actually made not with plums but raisins!

I love to make the Fruited Scone recipe with raisins, golden raisins or glacé cherries. Traditional fruited scones would be made with golden raisins or raisins. When you add the flour, baking soda and sugar to the saucepan, mix in ½ cup of your chosen dried fruit and proceed with the Rich Scone recipe as normal.

WONDERFUL VARIATIONS

ORANGE-SCENTED SCONES

FUN FACT

These are a favorite at Kensington Palace and are served in the Orangery.

Using the Rich Scone recipe, add the grated zest of one orange to the flour mixture and create your scones. The zesty fragrance will fill your kitchen!

WONDERFUL VARIATIONS

CHEESE SCONES

30 Min

FUN FACT

There are over 700 kinds of British cheese, most of which are from England. Probably the most famous is Cheddar which was created in the 1100s. It takes its name from the caves in which the cheese was stored, Cheddar Gorge, in Somerset, in the West of England.

King Henry II bought 4.6 tons of Cheddar in 1170 and declared the cheese to be the best in Britain!

I love these cheese scones with just butter. Using the Rich Scone recipe, replace the sugar with a 1 cup of grated cheese and bake in the usual way. I would recommend Cheddar, but any hard flavorsome cheese would work very well. They will need more like 12 minutes in the oven to be cooked throughout, as the cheese needs to be melted and incorporated into the scone.

These are delicious straight out of the oven split in half and buttered or allow to cool and topped with butter and a savory topping of your choice.

DROPPED SCONES

30 Min

These are some of my favorite scones. I remember cooking these as part of my Food and Nutrition exam, and forced to eat the ones that weren't perfectly round! But no exam here - so any shape will be wonderful!

These use a batter that you "drop" onto a griddle, or fry pan on the stove to cook. It is a bit misleading to call them dropped for you actually sort of blob them out. However, you get the idea that no oven is needed for this recipe. Nor do they need to be perfectly round! They are a little like small pancakes.

FUN FACT

Her Majesty Queen Elizabeth II made Dropped Scones for President Dwight Eisenhower when he visited Balmoral castle in 1959. Later she sent the President a letter and enclosed the recipe, with annotations and a suggestion to use treacle or molasses in place of the superfine sugar.

INGREDIENTS (MAKES 10)

1 cup self-rising flour

1 tablespoon butter

2 tablespoons superfine sugar or 2 tablespoons molasses

1 egg

½ cup milk

METHOD

1. Melt the butter.

2. Measure out the flour and sugar or molasses into a bowl and pour in the egg, milk and melted butter.

3. Mix together with a whisk. You get a thick batter, a bit thicker than American pancake batter.

4. Drop a tablespoon of batter onto your hot griddle or fry pan. Continue with separate tablespoons of batter to fill up your fry pan, perhaps about 5 and cook for about 3 minutes.

5. You will know when to flip your scones as tiny little bubbles appear on the surface. Turn them over and cook for 2 minutes on the other side.

6. Eat hot with butter or leave to cool and eat with butter and a sweet topping of your choice.

WONDERFUL VARIATIONS

Drop a few raisins onto each scone while it is cooking. Or mix in a ½ cup into the batter before you begin. You could even use chocolate chips!

CONCLUDING REMARKS

The Rich Scones look so-impressive topped with preserves and cream. The taste will not disappoint you either! Even the Queen of England enjoys a good Dropped Scone.

I haven't mentioned cakes yet, but tea and cake are a heavenly combination! The following cake recipes are so easy because they are created in a saucepan with melted butter, and put straight into a cake pan and into the oven. I can guarantee you will never want to use a packet mix again!

CAKES

INTRODUCTION

Creating your own cake from scratch is so impressive and yet with these recipes so easy! In fact it's just as easy as a packet mix, but without the additional chemicals - which you can do without! Any of these recipes will give you a delicious home-made cake with very little effort.

A quick word on ensuring that your cake emerges from its pan in one piece. You can, of course cut out parchment paper and line your pan. I find this a bit time-consuming when I want to get on with baking. You can also buy ready-made parchment liners that are the correct shape for your pan, which really work well.

If you don't have any parchment paper, thoroughly grease the pan with butter or a little oil on the sides and bottom, and then add a tablespoon of flour and coat the greased pan by tipping and jostling the flour over every inch of the pan and then tip out what is leftover. Any area left uncoated could be the sight of a "cake-stick" incident. Afterward, not only do you feel as dexterous as Mrs Patmore, from Downton Abbey but just as important, you are providing a barrier to stop the cake mix from bonding to the sides of your pan. It has never failed me.

ROUND

THE VICTORIA SANDWICH CAKE

This is quintessentially English. It is a sponge cake and traditionally filled with only raspberry preserve and dusted with superfine sugar. Actually, I think it tastes rather better if you add some butter frosting in the middle as well, which is how it is now usually served.

FUN FACT
This cake was Queen Victoria's favorite but originally was invented for her children at Osborne House on the Isle of Wight, just off the south coast of England.

INGREDIENTS
Cake
1 cup (or 2 sticks) butter
1 teaspoon vanilla extract
1 cup superfine sugar
2 ¼ cups self-rising flour
1 teaspoon baking soda
4 large eggs

2x 8" round cake pans.

Vanilla Frosting

½ cup (or 1 stick) butter

½ teaspoon vanilla extract

1 tablespoon milk

2 ½ cups powdered sugar

Raspberry Filling

Half of a 13oz jar of raspberry preserves

1-2 tablespoons of superfine sugar for sprinkling on top.

METHOD FOR THE CAKES

1. Pre-heat the oven to 350° F.

2. Melt the butter in a 3- or 4-quart saucepan. Leave to one side.

3. Prepare your round cake pans, by lining with parchment paper or by greasing and flouring them.

4. Add vanilla extract, sugar, flour and baking soda to the melted butter. Make a well and add the eggs.

5. Mix briskly together. It will begin to rise straight-away - but don't worry.

6. Immediately tip half of the mixture into each prepared pan and place them in the oven for about 20-25 minutes.

7. They are ready when they are golden, and spring back a little when touched.

8. Remove from the pans and leave to cool while you make the frosting.

METHOD FOR THE FROSTING

1. Melt the butter in a 3-quart saucepan and add the powdered sugar, vanilla extract and milk. Beat together with a wooden spoon. If it is too runny, add a little more powdered sugar, if too thick add a little more milk until it looks like frosting.

2. When the cakes are cool, spread raspberry preserve over one of the cakes and the vanilla frosting over the other and sandwich together.

3. Sprinkle with superfine sugar and you're done.

CAKE VARIATIONS

CHOCOLATE CAKE

Substitute ¼ cup of cocoa for the same quantity of flour and proceed with the recipe.

COFFEE CAKE

Add 4 level teaspoons of instant coffee, dissolved in 1 tablespoon of hot water to the melted butter and proceed with the recipe.

WONDERFUL VARIATIONS

FROSTING VARIATIONS

CHOCOLATE FUDGE FROSTING

INGREDIENTS

½ cup (or 1 stick) butter

1 teaspoon vanilla extract

2 tablespoons cocoa

3 cups powdered sugar

3 tablespoons milk

METHOD

1. Melt the butter in a 3-quart saucepan and mix in the vanilla extract

2. Add the cocoa, powdered sugar and milk and beat until smooth.

This should be plenty to fill and frost your cake.

COFFEE FROSTING

As for Vanilla Frosting, but instead of the vanilla extract and the milk, just dissolve 2 teaspoons of instant coffee in 1 tablespoon of hot water.

FRUIT CAKE

This fruit cake is light, moist and crumbly. It is not at all dense or heavy. If you haven't tried this before, I encourage you to try baking some. It also fills the kitchen with such a lovely aroma while baking.

FUN FACT

The ancient Egyptians made fruit cake for their departed loved ones to carry with them into the afterlife. Returning Crusaders brought fruit with them by drying or candying the fruit for travel, and, when the fruit reached Northern Europe, it was shared by mixing it in breads and cakes.

Queen Victoria served a single layer fruit cake at her Wedding to Prince Albert. Fruit cake was served at Princess Diana's Wedding to Prince Charles and more recently at Prince William and Kate's Wedding.

INGREDIENTS

2 ½ cups mixed fruit (I like a mixture of 1 cup raisins, 1 cup golden raisins and ½ cup currants)
½ cup (or 1 stick) butter
½ cup soft brown sugar
⅔ cup water
2 cups self-rising flour
1 egg

One 6" or 7" round cake pan

METHOD

1. Pre-heat the oven to 300° F.

2. Place fruit, butter, sugar and half of the water in a 3- or 4-quart saucepan. Heat until the butter has melted and then remove from the heat. Some of the water added at this stage is partially absorbed by the fruit to make it juicier.

3. Add the remaining water - this will cool the mixture down a little as you don't want it too hot or else most of the rising will be done before the cake gets into the oven!

4. Set aside and while it is cooling, prepare your cake pan, either by inserting the correct ready formed parchment paper shape for your pan or greasing and flouring as described above.

5. Add the flour to the pan, make a well and add the egg. Mix briskly together. It will begin to rise straight-away - but don't worry.

6. Immediately tip the mixture into your prepared pan and place in the oven for about 50 minutes - 1 hour.

7. Leave to cool in the pan so that it retains its shape.

WONDERFUL VARIATIONS

CHERRY CAKE

FUN FACT:

The Romans used to preserve fruit using honey over 2000 years ago. Glacé cherries have existed since at least the 1300s in a little town called Apt, in Provence, France. The process of saturating the cherries with sugar was used to preserve the fruit. In 1868, an Englishman named Matthew Wood discovered the local specialty and helped introduce French Glacé Cherries to the English market. Glacé cherries have been enjoyed in our fruit cakes ever since.

Seeing the crimson cherries nestled in your cake when you cut into it, is quite lovely.

Replace the mixed fruit with 2 cups of chopped glacé cherries.

WONDERFUL VARIATIONS

DATE AND ORANGE

FUN FACT:
There is evidence of dates from about 4000 BC in Ur but they seem to have first arrived in England in the early medieval period. Sugar was expensive and so by 1660s dates were being used in all sorts of dishes, from sauces for meat to salads.

To make a date and orange cake, replace the dried fruit with 2 cups of chopped dates and the zest of one orange.

CONCLUDING REMARKS

The Victoria Sandwich Cake or any of the other fruited whole round cakes makes a wonderful sight. You can dust with powdered sugar if the cake doesn't have its own topping, or leave majestic in its golden baked glory.

I shall next set out some easy Square Cakes. Square Cakes are baked in one pan as they are single layered. They cut easily into squares or can be decorated as one wonderful square cake. You will find recipes for Old-Fashioned Lemon Gingerbread, a Rich Chocolate Cake and a Medieval Honey Cake, inspired by the spices brought back from the Crusades topped with Earl Grey Tea Frosting.

SQUARE

OLD-FASHIONED LEMON GINGERBREAD

FUN FACT:

Queen Elizabeth I is said to have created the Gingerbread Man and presented her courtiers with gingerbread likenesses of themselves in the late 1500s. Of course, ginger is fabulously good for you as well. Antibacterial properties and aiding digestion are just two of the many health benefits. But the real reason for cooking with ginger is its delicious flavor.

This wonderful, damp and aromatic gingerbread is cake-like, rather than the cookie/biscuit variety. It is flavored with the sunshine of lemons which has been used in gingerbread for hundreds of years.

INGREDIENTS

- 1 cup (or 2 sticks) butter
- ¼ cup honey
- ½ cup molasses
- 1 cup brown sugar
- ¼ cup milk
- ¼ cup lemon juice
- 2 large eggs
- 1 teaspoon mixed spice or pumpkin spice
- 4 teaspoons ginger
- ½ teaspoon ground nutmeg
- zest of 2 lemons
- 2 ½ cups self-rising flour
- 9" square pan

METHOD

1. Heat the oven to 325° F.

2. Melt together the butter, honey and molasses in a 3- or 4-quart saucepan until the butter has just finished melting.

3. Remove from the heat and prepare your pan, thus giving your buttery mixture a little time to cool.

4. Add the brown sugar to the saucepan and stir.

5. Beat in the cold milk, lemon juice and the eggs and spices.

6. Whisk in the flour and lemon zest and mix well. It will be rather runny, but that is perfect.

7. Pour into the prepared pan and bake for about 50-55 minutes until springy to the touch, bearing in mind it will continue to cook in the pan.

8. Leave to cool for 5 minutes before tipping out of the pan to cool on a cooling rack.

To decorate, either cover with a dusting of powdered sugar or spread over the cake some lemon glacé frosting. Mix 5 ⅓ cups of powdered sugar with 8 tablespoons of lemon juice. It should be fairly thick to spread on top of your cake. Leave the frosting to set before serving.

RICH CHOCOLATE CAKE

FUN FACT:

Chocolate became very popular at the court of King Charles II in the 1650s in London as a drink. It was rather bitter, but in the 1700s, the English improved it by adding milk.

The chocolate ganache frosting could not be easier! You simply melt the chocolate in hot cream. It sounds so impressive though! As a variation, you could add some orange zest to the ganache.

INGREDIENTS

1 cup dark chocolate chips

1 cup (or 2 sticks) butter

1 cup superfine sugar

4 large eggs

2 cups self-rising flour

9" square pan

METHOD

1. Heat the oven to 325° F.

2. Melt the butter and chocolate together in a 3- or 4-quart saucepan and set aside.

3. Prepare your pan.

4. Beat in the sugar and the eggs.

5. Fold in the flour.

6. Pour into your prepared pan and bake in the oven for about 35 minutes until it is springy to the touch.

7. Leave to cool and then frost with the chocolate ganache.

CHOCOLATE GANACHE

INGREDIENTS

2 cups dark chocolate chips
1 cup heavy cream

METHOD

1. Heat the cream to nearly boiling in a 2-quart saucepan and remove from the heat.

2. Tip in the chopped chocolate chips and mix until chocolate has melted. If the chocolate is too large, it won't melt before the cream cools. If that happens, heat the saucepan a little so the chocolate melts.

3. Once it has cooled and is thick enough (you may need to put it in the fridge), spread it over your cake and decorate in whatever way you like, with flakes of chocolate or chocolate buttons.

MEDIEVAL HONEY CAKE WITH EARL GREY TEA FROSTING

FUN FACT

Honey bees have been kept for thousands of years in England. Honey would have been known to any cook in the great English country houses. In the year 1265, it is recorded that Eleanor, Countess of Leicester, used honey extensively in cooking at Dover Castle.

Inspired by this, I have created this Medieval Honey Cake using honey and some of the spices brought back during the Crusades. It is moist and flavorsome and somehow transports me back to the age of Chivalry. Topped with the Earl Grey Tea Frosting, this cake has a wonderful hint of smokey bergamot.

INGREDIENTS

⅔ cup butter
¾ cup honey
¾ cup brown sugar
2 tablespoons milk
3 large eggs
2 teaspoons cinnamon
2 teaspoons coriander
¼ teaspoon cloves
¼ teaspoon ground nutmeg
2 ½ cups self-rising flour
1 teaspoon baking soda

9" square pan

EARL GREY TEA FROSTING

INGREDIENTS

6 tablespoons of hot Earl Grey Tea

2 tablespoons honey

5 1/3 cups powdered sugar

METHOD

1. Heat the oven to 325° F.

2. Melt together the butter and honey in a 3- or 4-quart saucepan so the butter has just melted.

3. Remove from the heat and prepare your pan, thus giving your buttery mixture a little time to cool.

4. Add the brown sugar to the saucepan and stir.

5. Beat in the cold milk and the eggs and spices.

6. Whisk in the flour and baking soda and mix well. It will be rather runny, but that is perfect.

7. Pour into the prepared pan and bake for about 50-55 minutes until springy to the touch, bearing in mind it will continue to cook in the pan.

8. Leave to cool in the pan.

To decorate, either cover with a dusting of powdered sugar or cover with Earl Grey Tea frosting.

To make the Earl Grey Tea frosting, mix 5 ⅓ cups of powdered sugar with 2 tablespoons of honey and 6 tablespoons hot Earl Grey Tea. You want the frosting to have a fairly thick consistency to spread on top of your cake. Add a little more hot Earl Grey Tea ¼ teaspoon at a time if you want to drizzle the frosting across the cake.

CONCLUDING REMARKS

These recipes for Square Cakes are very versatile and can be served in chunks or as a whole cake frosted and looking gorgeous. Loaf and Rock cakes are next. The loaf cakes are sliced and can be eaten as they are or with added butter spread on top for extra creaminess. The recipes include Teabread which actually uses tea in the bread, date and walnut loaf and one of my favorites, caraway seed and apple loaf. The caraway seeds give such a wonderful scent!

LOAF AND ROCK

TEABREAD

Now, Teabread actually does use tea and it adds an exotic twist to this fat-free bread. Having said that it's fat-free, it usually isn't by the time it gets to your mouth! That's because once it's baked and sliced, you add your own butter to it! It has a slight crispiness on the outside and a chewy sweetness inside which reacts beautifully with slightly salty butter. I defy anyone not to be delighted with this!

FUN FACT
Iced tea was first served during a heatwave at the St Louis World Fair in 1904.

INGREDIENTS
⅓ cup hot tea
1½ cups golden raisins
¾ cup raisins
¾ cup currants
1 cup demerara sugar
⅓ cup cold water
1 large egg
1 ½ cups self-rising flour

2lb loaf pan

METHOD

1. Put the oven on at 300° F.

2. To make the tea, put about ½ cup of almost boiling water in a cup and add 1 tea bag and leave to brew for 3 minutes.

3. While the tea is brewing, measure out all the dried fruit and place it in the 3- or 4-quart saucepan, with the sugar and ⅓ cup hot tea. Warm through. The idea is that the fruit will absorb some of the tea and the sugar will dissolve.

4. Remove from the heat and add the ⅓ cup cold water to slightly cool down the mixture.

5. Grease and flour the loaf pan.

6. I can't wait for everything to cool down, so tip the flour and baking soda into the saucepan and make a well in the middle and add the egg.

7. Mix everything together, briskly, and because it is warm, the raising agent will immediately start to work. That's fine.

8. Tip into the prepared loaf pan and then put it straight into the oven for about 1 hour.

9. When cooked, leave to cool in the pan.

Serve when cold, thinly sliced and spread with butter.

DATE AND WALNUT LOAF

FUN FACT

The Romans called walnuts, "Jupiter's Royal Acorn".

INGREDIENTS

½ cup (or 1 stick) butter

¾ cup water

1 cup chopped pitted dates

1 teaspoon baking soda

1¼ cups brown sugar

2 cups self-rising flour

½ cup chopped walnuts

1 egg

2lb loaf pan

METHOD

1. Heat the oven to 325° F.

2. Melt the butter together with the water, chopped dates and baking soda in a 3- or 4-quart saucepan.

3. Prepare your loaf pan.

4. Add the brown sugar, flour and walnuts to the buttery dates and beat in the egg.

5. Place the batter into the loaf pan and bake for 55 minutes or until when you touch the surface it no longer wobbles.

6. Leave to cool in the pan.

Serve as it is, or spread with butter.

APPLE AND SEED CAKE

FUN FACT

Caraway seeds have been used for thousands of years. They are mentioned in Shakespeare's Henry IV Part Two along with Pippin apples, " ...last year's pippin of my own graffing, with a dish of caraways."

Inspired by Shakespeare, I have created this apple and seed cake. I love the combination. There is no need to peel the apples - the skin disappears in the cooking process - amazing!

INGREDIENTS

½ cup (or 1 stick) butter

¼ cup water

2 cups chopped apples, (about 2 small apples) no need to peel

1 teaspoon baking soda

1 ½ cups brown sugar

2 cups self-rising flour

1 tablespoon caraway seeds

1 egg

2lb loaf pan

METHOD

1. Heat the oven to 325° F.

2. Melt the butter together with the water, chopped apples and baking soda in a 3- or 4-quart saucepan and leave to one side.

3. Prepare your loaf pan.

4. Add the brown sugar, flour and caraway seeds to the buttery apples and beat in the egg.

5. Place the batter into the loaf pan and bake for 55 minutes until springy to the touch.

6. Allow to cool in the pan so that it retains its shape.

Serve as it is, or spread with butter.

ROCK CAKES

30 Min

You will be glad to know the name does not refer to the hardness of these little cakes, but to their resemblance to rocks! They are a curious hybrid of scones and butter cakes. The resulting taste is absolutely delicious. If you think you don't like dried fruit in cakes - this will change your mind! There is something amazing that seems to happen in the alchemy of these wonderful cakes!

FUN FACT

Originally invented by the Victorians, during the Second World War, the UK Ministry of Food promoted Rock Cakes because they contain less butter and sugar than ordinary cakes. It is amazing that they taste so good. They have been the mainstay of English village fetes since the Victorian era.

INGREDIENTS

½ cup (or 1 stick) butter
⅓ cup superfine sugar
2 cups self-rising flour
⅔ cup dried fruit (say ⅓ cup currants and ⅓ cup raisins)
1 egg
1 tablespoon milk to mix

Superfine sugar to sprinkle over.

METHOD

1. Heat the oven to 400° F.

2. Melt the butter in a 3- or 4-quart saucepan.

3. Prepare your cookie sheets by covering with parchment paper.

4. Add all the other dry ingredients and the egg to the saucepan and mix thoroughly.

5. Dollop out onto the prepared baking sheet in mounds to look like rocks about the size of a large golf ball.

6. Place in the oven for about 14-15 minutes.

7. Once they are out of the oven sprinkle superfine sugar on top.

CONCLUDING REMARKS

By this point, you have some wonderful options for scones and cakes of many different varieties. But what about something with a different texture from a cake? Let me introduce the biscuit. Very different from the American biscuit, a little more like a cookie, the English biscuit is usually crunchy or melting.

The following section includes a variety of biscuits and shortbreads. I am particularly fond of the mixed spice snaps, and the orange-scented shortbread - they could be ready in 30 minutes.

BISCUITS

INTRODUCTION

English biscuits are unlike any American biscuit. Don't get me wrong, I love the fluffy light American biscuits, but the recipes that follow are not trying to be that. Also, they're not trying to be cookies. I have included two types of biscuit: one that is crunchy and snaps when you break it and another that has a more melting, shortbread texture. I hope these recipes will introduce you to a new type of treat that will surprise you and that you will want to make over and over again.

The English Courts have spent quite some time and money examining the very issue of how to define a biscuit! The case involved the tax authorities and McVities, who make Jaffa Cakes. Is the Jaffa Cake a cake or a biscuit? If it was a cake, no tax was payable, but if a biscuit - then bad news for McVities!

The Court decided that when a cake is left in the open, it dries out and hardens, but when a biscuit is left, it softens. You'll be glad to know that the Jaffa Cake was found really to be a cake as it dries out when left exposed to the air. So that's it! Now you know! When making these biscuits, I've never had the chance to see whether they soften when left out, as they are devoured too quickly!

The word "biscuit" comes from the Latin - meaning twice-baked. Though all these recipes only get one blast in the oven!

Dunking a biscuit in some kind of liquid can be traced back to King Richard I of England. He left for the Third Crusade in 1189 with "biskit of muslin," which was a mixed grain compound of barley, bean flour, and rye. It was so hard that he had to dunk it so that it was soft enough to eat!

In the year of 1492, Christopher Columbus and his sailors would have eaten ships biscuits on board the Santa Maria. These biscuits would have lasted a year or more if kept dry.

I've kept to my guarantee that you will need no electric mixers or food gadgets, no rubbing in and no rolling out. In fact, all of these biscuit recipes are 30 minutes from measure to munch and you'll have time to have a quick cuppa while the biscuits are cooking!

SNAPPY

GINGER SNAPS

30 Min

FUN FACT

Even Shakespeare understood the importance of ginger. As Costard said in Love's Labor's Lost, "An I had but one penny in the world, thou should'st have it to buy gingerbread."

These biscuits, as you may have guessed from the title, are the crunchy, snappy kind. One tip for measuring out honey - oil the inside of your measuring cup, then pour in the honey, it will come out without sticking.

INGREDIENTS

½ cup (or 1 stick) butter

¼ cup honey - this should be clear, runny honey

1 tablespoon ginger powder

1 ⅓ cups light brown sugar

2 ⅓ cups self-rising flour

1 large egg

Cookie Sheets.

METHOD

1. Preheat the oven to 350° F.

2. Place butter, honey and ginger in a 3- or 4-quart saucepan and warm through so the butter has just melted. In fact, I turn off the heat just before the butter has finished melting, as you want the mixture to be a cool as possible.

3. Put to one side while you prepare your cookie sheets - I say prepare, but all you need to do is take some parchment paper about the size of your sheets and lay it on top - no greasing.

4. Add the brown sugar to the saucepan and mix in.

5. Add the flour and egg. Mix well.

6. Take a teaspoon of the mixture, roll into a ball with your hands and place it on your prepared cookie sheet. Place three fingers on the ball and press down to slightly flatten it. Place more balls about 1 inch apart, as they will spread a little during the cooking process. This makes about 30-36.

7. Bake these in the oven for about 13-15 minutes, until golden brown.

Leave them on the sheet for a few minutes before transferring them to a cooling rack. When cold they will be snappy. They are lovely just munched, or perfect for dunking in tea as they soften beautifully.

WONDERFUL VARIATIONS

MIXED SPICE BISCUITS

30 Min

FUN FACT

Mixed Spice is an English invention and rather like pumpkin spice. It usually contains a mixture of cinnamon, coriander, nutmeg, ginger, and cloves. Though used in cookbooks since 1828, it was a prized possession much earlier. These spices were very costly during the height of the East India Company.

Just replace the ginger with Mixed Spice and make in the same way as the Ginger Snap recipe.

WONDERFUL VARIATIONS

TOFFEE CRUNCH BISCUITS

FUN FACT

Demerara sugar is so-called because it originally came from sugar cane fields in Demerara on the north coast of South America.

These biscuits have a little toffee crunch in them because of the added demerara sugar.

Add ¼ cup demerara sugar with the self-rising flour and continue with the Ginger Snap recipe leaving out the ginger.

TREACLE OATIES

30 Min

FUN FACT

Using black treacle or molasses gives these oat biscuits a dark richness and depth of flavor, and along with the oats gives them a firmer texture. A tip to avoid making a sticky molasses mess is to oil the inside of the measuring cup before measuring out the molasses. They will then come out in a blob straight into the pan.

INGREDIENTS

¼ cup (or ½ stick) butter
¼ cup soft brown sugar
¼ cup molasses
½ cup all-purpose flour
1 cup oats
½ teaspoon baking soda

Cookie Sheet

METHOD

1. Preheat the oven to 350° F.

2. Place the butter and molasses into a 3- or 4-quart saucepan and warm through so the butter is almost melted.

3. Then remove from the heat for the butter to finish melting, as you want the mixture to be as cool as possible.

4. Put to one side while you prepare your cookie sheets by placing the parchment paper on them.

5. Add the soft brown sugar to the saucepan and stir.

6. Add the flour, oats and baking soda. Mix well. If it is too sticky add another tablespoon of oats until firm enough to handle. Makes about 10.

7. Use your hands to squeeze together about a teaspoonful of mixture into a ball, place on the sheet and squash flat with your fingers, about 1 inch apart and continue until you have used up all the mixture.

8. Bake these in the oven for about 12 minutes. They should be darker and look crispy on top when cooked. Leave on the sheet for a few minutes before transferring them to a cooling tray.

SHORTBREAD

INDIVIDUAL RICH SHORTBREADS

30 Min

This is a wonderfully buttery, melting kind of biscuit. The rubbing in method is usually used for shortbread, but it works beautifully for this one pan method. By adding the cornstarch as a replacement for some of the flour, you get a more melting texture.

FUN FACT

Until 1851, cornstarch was used only in starching laundry!

INGREDIENTS

1 cup (or 2 sticks) butter

1 teaspoon vanilla extract

1 cup powdered sugar

¾ cup cornstarch

1 ¾ cups all-purpose flour

Superfine sugar to sprinkle.

METHOD

1. Preheat the oven to 350° F.

2. Place butter in a 3- or 4-quart saucepan and warm through so the butter is almost melted.

3. Remove from the heat and add the vanilla extract.

4. Put the saucepan to one side while you prepare your cookie sheet. Place a sheet of parchment paper over the cookie sheet. There is no need to butter it since there's plenty of butter in the mixture.

5. Add the powdered sugar, cornstarch and flour to the saucepan and mix together, gently. You do not want to handle this too much or else the texture will be too doughy.

6. Take a teaspoon of mixture and place it on the prepared sheet. Continue until all the mixture is used.

7. Form each blob of mixture into a rough ball with your hands.

8. Use three fingers to press down each ball. Then mark each ball with the back of a fork. This makes 20-24 depending on their size.

9. Bake in the oven for about 12 minutes. They should be a pale golden brown when cooked.

10. Leave to cool on the cookie sheets because they are quite fragile until cool.

WONDERFUL VARIATIONS

CUSTARD SHORTBREAD

30 Min

FUN FACT

Custard has been made in England for hundreds of years. Traditionally, it is made with milk, sugar and eggs and is a sweet sauce poured over hot desserts. An easy way of making custard was invented in 1837 and was an immediate hit. It is still made today and sold as Bird's custard powder. So important is custard to the English palate that it was supplied to the British Armed Forces during World War 1!

Just substitute the cornstarch for ¾ cup of custard powder. This is the unsweetened Bird's custard powder, not the instant custard which contains sugar. If it is not available in your local store, it is available online. The emerging shortbreads are more yellow and have a melting creamy flavor.

WONDERFUL VARIATIONS

SESAME COVERED SHORTBREAD

FUN FACT

When sesame seed pods are ripe, they burst open releasing their seeds. It is thought that this is why in the story of "Ali Baba and the Forty Thieves" a sealed cave magically opens with the phrase "Open Sesame!"

Roll each ball in sesame seeds before baking. Continue to press down slightly with your fingers and impress with the fork once on the cookie sheet.

WONDERFUL VARIATIONS

CARAWAY SHORTBREAD

30 Min

FUN FACT

Caraway seeds were used in love potions to help a lover stay true. They were sometimes given to chickens to stop them from wandering away from home, and also given to homing pigeons so they didn't stray too far.

They became very popular in Queen Victoria's reign in the 1800s. Like ginger, they have some medicinal use as an aid to digestion, and have antiseptic properties also.

Whether you wish to keep a love, or just love the flavor, add 1 tablespoon of caraway seeds along with the flour.

WONDERFUL VARIATIONS

LAVENDER SHORTBREAD

English lavender is perfect for baking as it has a sweet mellowness to it.

FUN FACT

So the story goes, Queen Elizabeth I insisted that a jar of Lavender preserve be available for every meal.

Add 1 teaspoon of dried lavender buds along with the flour to evoke the scent of the English country gardens of yesteryear.

WONDERFUL VARIATIONS

ORANGE-SCENTED SHORTBREAD

FUN FACT

Oranges are unknown in the wild, but were apparently developed and cultivated first in China. Did the word "orange" first come to describe the fruit or the color? "Orange" was actually first used as the name of the fruit and later became the term used for the color.

Add the grated zest of one orange along with the flour.

WONDERFUL VARIATIONS

ALMOND SHORTBREAD

30 Min

FUN FACT

The Romans first brought almonds to England. Almonds were used extensively in cooking in medieval times and grown all over England.

Replace the vanilla extract with 1 teaspoon of almond extract and add ¼ cup of ground almonds. I like to top these with some chopped almonds before baking and then sprinkle over the superfine sugar when they emerge, fragrant, from the oven!

WONDERFUL VARIATIONS

CHOCOLATE SHORTBREAD

FUN FACT

In 1847, the first chocolate bar was invented by the Fry Company in England.

Replace ¼ cup of flour with cocoa.

DECORATIONS FOR YOUR BISCUITS

All these biscuits look beautiful, but here are a few options if you are feeling like jazzing them up.

DUST WITH POWDERED SUGAR

Simply arrange your biscuits on a plate and push a little icing sugar through a tea strainer - if you don't have one - use a sieve. This makes any biscuit look delicious, and who can refuse a little extra sweetening in their life?

EASY GLACÉ FROSTING

Make a little glacé icing and drizzle across your biscuit. You can even make up 2 colors for extra effect.

Mix 1 ⅓ cups of powdered sugar and 2 tablespoons of warm water together. Add ¼ teaspoon of water at a time to get the desired drizzling consistency. With the biscuits still on their cooling rack, drizzle the frosting using teaspoonfuls of frosting in sweeping movements across the biscuits, Jackson Pollock-like.

Once you have decorated in one direction, repeat at right angles to get a crisscross effect.

You can decorate each one individually if the mood takes you - but this is quick and effective. I like the random nature of the drizzled frosting.

CONCLUDING REMARKS

This section has given you lots of different types of biscuits that can be created very simply. Next I would like to broaden the teatime treat recipes to include treats inspired from around the world. The English have always absorbed great ideas from other countries and food is no exception. These recipes add an exotic flavor to the tea table, but of course, they are so easy to make!

INTRODUCTION

Each of these recipes is inspired from the countries that have influenced England or were part of the British Empire. You will find flavors ranging from chili chocolate crispies to lavender marshmallow squares inspired from ancient Egypt.

TIFFIN

INTRODUCTION
Tiffin comes from the days of the British Raj in India. Tiffin is very easy as there is no baking at all, only a little melting on the stove and chilling in the fridge required. What a wonderful invention this is - the melding together and enrobing of biscuits in a buttery chocolate cloak!

FUN FACT
The word tiffin eventually was used to describe afternoon tea in the British Raj. The English in India borrowed "tiffing," an old English dialect or slang word for taking a little drink or sip, and used it to describe the afternoon tea.

INGREDIENTS
1 cup (or 2 sticks) butter
½ cup soft brown sugar
½ cup honey
½ cup cocoa
2 ⅔ cups Graham Crackers

9" square pan, lined with parchment paper.

TOPPING

1 ½ cups chocolate chips melted with 2 tablespoons butter.

METHOD

1. Melt the butter, sugar, honey and cocoa in a 3- or 4-quart saucepan.

2. Prepare your pan, by lining with parchment paper or foil.

3. Crush the crackers with your hands, some bigger chunks are really good, add to the saucepan and mix well. You want the crackers to be completely encased in the chocolatey mixture.

4. Tip out into your prepared pan and press down so the surface is flat.

5. Give your saucepan a quick rinse out and melt the chocolate chips with the butter. Be gentle with the chocolate as you don't want it overcooked, but just melted, so have it over a low heat.

6. Pour over the tiffin base and spread out.

7. Put in the fridge to chill for a couple of hours, then slice up and serve.

WONDERFUL VARIATIONS

You can add ½ cup of raisins, chopped apricots or chopped almonds for a variation, or even little marshmallows.

FLAPJACKS

INTRODUCTION

The English Flapjack is a completely different thing from the American Flapjack. The English Flapjack is made using oats, butter, sugar and Golden Syrup. Golden Syrup is widely available in England, and is rather like the American Corn Syrup. I have replaced Golden Syrup with honey because it has a far longer cooking tradition and is far better for you!

These are very simple, quick and delicious as the butter, honey and sugar combine to make a toffee caramel mixture to which you add the oats. You are looking for the rolled whole porridge oats here, not the instant ones, as it's the whole oats that create a firm, crispy outside but leave the center soft and sweet. You and your guests can indulge yourselves in the natural sweet goodness of honey and feel virtuous because of the oats. It is the variations that embrace the exotic.

FUN FACT

Each morning, the breakfast table of Her Majesty Queen Elizabeth II includes porridge oats in a Tupperware container!

Porridge oats are the main ingredient in the following recipe for flapjacks.

RICH FLAPJACKS

30 Min

INGREDIENTS
1 cup (or 2 sticks) butter
1 cup soft brown sugar
1 cup clear runny honey
4 cups porridge oats
9" square pan, lined with parchment paper.

METHOD
1. Preheat the oven to 350° F.

2. Prepare your pan. Simply take some parchment paper and cut a length that will cover it. No need to grease as there is plenty of butter in this recipe.

3. Add the butter, sugar and honey to a 3- or 4-quart saucepan and heat until the butter has melted and the mixture is bubbling.

4. Add the oats and thoroughly mix together.

5. Bake for about 20-25 minutes. You want the mixture to be bubbling around the sides, and crispy on top, but to still maintain its squishiness in the middle. Leave for 2 minutes before cutting into squares, but leave to cool in the pan or else they will fall apart!

Really, you can vary these however you fancy. I've included a few of my favorites like the apricot, almond and cardamom flapjacks, inspired from India.

WONDERFUL VARIATIONS

GINGER OR CINNAMON FLAPJACKS

Just add 2 teaspoons of spice to the mixture before you add the oats and mix thoroughly.

WONDERFUL VARIATIONS

CHOCOLATE FLAPJACKS

30 Min

Add 2 tablespoons of cocoa to the mixture before you add the oats and mix thoroughly. You could also drizzle over a little melted chocolate when they have cooled.

WONDERFUL VARIATIONS

DATE, CHERRY OR RAISIN FLAPJACKS

Add 1 cup of dried fruit before you add the oats and mix thoroughly.

WONDERFUL VARIATIONS

APRICOT, ALMOND AND CARDAMOM FLAPJACKS

Add ½ cup of chopped dried apricots, ¼ cup of chopped almonds and ¼ teaspoon of ground cardamom to the mixture before you add the oats, and mix thoroughly. Bake these for about 25 minutes. The scent of cardamom is very evocative of India.

ORANGE-SCENTED ALMOND MACAROONS

30 Min

FUN FACT

In 1259, ground almonds only cost about 3 cents per pound! Macaroons probably originated in an Italian monastery in the 800s AD. There are many variations, but all recipes use ground almonds, sugar and egg whites. Sometimes the egg whites are whipped, but there is no need to do that here.

INGREDIENTS (MAKES ABOUT 25)

3 cups ground almonds
1 cup superfine sugar
zest of 2 oranges
2 egg whites
1 tablespoon orange juice
Blanched almonds to decorate

Cookie sheets.

METHOD

1. Heat the oven to 400° F.

2. Prepare the cookie sheets by greasing, or lay some parchment paper on them.

3. Mix the ground almonds, sugar, orange zest, egg whites and orange juice together in a bowl with a fork.

4. Take a teaspoon size of the mixture and place it on the parchment sheet, continue until all the mixture is used.

5. Form each blob of mixture into a rough ball with your fingers, slightly flatten and decorate with a blanched almond.

6. Bake for about 10-12 minutes until slightly brown.

COCONUT MACAROONS

30 Min

FUN FACT

The term "coco" is used in Spanish and Portuguese colloquial speech to refer to a human head or skull. If you hold the coconut so that you are looking at the three holes surrounded by the hairy husk, it does resemble a face!

INGREDIENTS (MAKES ABOUT 20)

2 cups desiccated unsweetened coconut

1 cup superfine sugar

2 egg whites

Pinch of salt

Glacé cherries to decorate.

METHOD

1. Heat the oven to 350° F.

2. Prepare cookie sheets by placing parchment paper over them.

3. In a bowl, mix all the ingredients, except the cherries together with a fork.

4. Take a teaspoon of the mixture and roll into a ball and place on the parchment paper. These do flatten and spread so space them out. No need to press them down.

5. Pop a little piece, say $\frac{1}{8}$ of a glacé cherry, on top of each to decorate.

6. Bake for about 14 minutes. They crisp up when out of the oven, but remain gooey in the middle. Leave to cool on the parchment paper, as they are quite fragile until cool.

LAVENDER MARSHMALLOW SQUARES

FUN FACT

Originally, marshmallows came from the mallow plant which grew in marshes in Egypt - hence the name marsh-mallow. Nowadays there is no mallow in our marshmallows.

The Marshmallow Squares were created by Malitta Jensen and Mildred Day 1939, in America. The original recipe appeared in 1941 on the box of Kellogg's Rice Krispies and it has never changed since then! I have added the heavenly scent of lavender, which brings this classic an English twist.

INGREDIENTS

3 tablespoons butter
4 cups Miniature Marshmallows
1 teaspoon lavender buds
6 cups crisped rice cereal

9" square pan

METHOD

1. In a large saucepan, melt butter over low heat. Add marshmallows and stir until completely melted.

2. Add the lavender and stir thoroughly. Remove from the heat.

3. Add the crisped rice cereal and stir until well coated.

4. Using a buttered spatula or wax paper, evenly press the mixture into the pan coated with parchment paper. Cool. Cut into 2-inch squares.

CHILI CHOCOLATE CRISPIES

FUN FACT
This recipe is inspired from the Mayans who first enjoyed cocoa. They crushed the cocoa bean and drank it with chili! The chili here is not fiery, but adds a little welcome warmth.

INGREDIENTS
½ cup (or 1 stick) butter
½ cup honey
½ cup superfine sugar
3 tablespoons cocoa
¾ teaspoon chili powder
4 cups corn flakes

A 12-hole muffin pan and paper inserts. This makes 12.

METHOD
1. Melt the butter, honey, and sugar together in a large saucepan.

2. Remove from the heat and add the cocoa and chili powder.

3. Add the cornflakes and mix so that each flake is covered in the chocolate mixture.

4. Spoon into the individual muffin papers and leave to cool.

EASY CREAM PUFFS

INTRODUCTION

Have you enjoyed a cream puff or a summer puff before? Cream puffs are Choux pastry puffs, filled with cream and topped with frosting. I shall set out a recipe for you to create those puffs, but very easily.

Normally, it would involve making Choux pastry, which originated from France, but I have a very simple short-cut!

Most cookery books will tell you that Choux pastry is easy to make. Well it is, if you want to use an electric mixer, or increase the size of your arm muscles, not to mention using a piping bag and have loads of washing up to do afterward. That doesn't sound easy to me!

The following recipe is so easy, no electric mixer, or exhausted muscles, and no fiddling with a piping bag! Just make the batter and cook in a mini muffin pan!

FUN FACT

My parents had the honor of attending one of Her Majesty Queen Elizabeth II's Garden Parties in Buckingham Palace Gardens one year. They kindly brought home for each of my sisters and me a tiny, beautiful chocolate eclair, wrapped in Buckingham Palace loo paper! It was delicious! So if it's English enough for the Queen's garden party then it's good enough for any occasion!

EASY CHOUX PASTRY

INGREDIENTS

3 tablespoons of vegetable oil

1 ⅓ cups all-purpose flour

⅔ cup milk

2 teaspoons vanilla extract

4 eggs

Frosting: 2 ⅔ cups powdered sugar.
Filling: Can of aerosol whipped cream.

24 hole mini muffin pan (no paper cases needed.)

METHOD

1. Pre-heat the oven to 350° F.

2. Pour a little oil into each mold of a 24-hole mini muffin pan and put in the oven until smoking hot.

3. Place the flour in a mixing bowl and make a well in the middle.

4. Add the milk, eggs and vanilla extract and whisk together with a balloon whisk. Leave to one side until the oil in the muffin pan is really hot.

5. Remove the muffin pan from the oven.

6. Carefully pour about a generous tablespoon of batter into each muffin hole until you have filled up all 24 of them.

7. Bake for 28-30 minutes. They should have all puffed up beautifully, and be golden brown.

Remove from the oven, pick each one up and turn over in the muffin pan to cool down.

Once cool, you are ready to frost and fill.

GLACÉ FROSTING

Mix 2 ⅔ cups of powdered sugar and 4 tablespoons of warm water together. That should be a good consistency, but if it is too stiff, add ¼ teaspoon of water at a time to get the desired consistency. Apply the frosting to the now top, that is the part that was cooked in the muffin pan. Leave to set. The reason for this upside-down maneuver is that the now bottom will have a little hole - just perfect for shooting in the cream.

FILLING

Only fill just before you want to eat. This is work of but a few moments. To fill, just shoot the cream in through the bottom of the pastry, if there is a hole, great, make use of that, if not, create a hole by inserting a small knife and twisting it round, then fill with cream.

WONDERFUL VARIATIONS

To vary the flavor of the puffs, change the frosting.

For chocolate puffs, add 2 tablespoons of cocoa to the frosting, for orange, add the zest of an orange and use 4 tablespoons of orange juice to mix with the powdered sugar and for raspberry, either top with a fresh or defrosted frozen raspberry, or sprinkle freeze-dried raspberries on top of your white frosting. Another delicious variation would be to top the puffs with powdered sugar mixed with Earl Grey Tea to create a smokey, bergamot flavor in the frosting.

CONCLUDING REMARKS

That was the exotic English afternoon tea treats. Those recipes add flavors absorbed into the English palate through long association with other countries. The next section involves cooking with yeast. There is just one recipe. But these Pikelets are so wonderful! Of course, there is very little effort involved for a fantastic result! No electric mixer and no need to knead!

OLD ENGLISH PIKELETS

INTRODUCTION

Now, I've promised you that it will be easy - so no kneading and no mixers involved. You may be thinking - but yeast cookery is all about kneading and proving and kneading again. Well, it usually is but not this time! It requires being left alone for about 1 hour, but no kneading. This is one of my family's favorite recipes - pikelets. What an amazing surprise these little bread/cakes are.

FUN FACT

Hieroglyphics show that yeast was used in Egyptian antiquity for baking bread. And archeologists have found stones used for baking bread as well as drawings for a 4000-year-old bakery. Leaven, referred to in the Bible, was a soft dough-like medium. A small portion of this dough was used to start or leaven each new batch of bread.

PIKELETS

You can eat these straight from the griddle covered in butter, or you can let them go cold and toast them and then add the butter. I can't seem to manage to wait until they get cold!

INGREDIENTS

2 ½ cups all-purpose flour
1 ½ cups cold milk mixed with
1 ½ cups hot water to make a nice warm mixture
1 heaped teaspoon, or a 7g packet of dried yeast
1 teaspoon of salt.

METHOD

1. Measure out the flour into a bowl.

2. Make a well in the middle and pour in some of the milk and water mixture. Whisk it together. The batter will be quite runny.

3. Tip in the yeast and whisk in.

4. Cover with a cloth and leave for about 1 hour, somewhere warm, until lots of bubbles have appeared on the surface.

5. Just before you are ready to cook the pikelets, whisk in the salt.

6. On a reasonably hot greased griddle, dollop spoonfuls of the batter. It doesn't matter if these are not perfectly round, but roundish is what you're aiming for.

7. Cook until bubbles appear on the top side, probably about 3 minutes then flip them - and cook for a minute or two until just solid and brown. Remove to a warm plate next to you.

8. Pile them up as you use all the mixture.

Butter them and eat hot or leave to go cold for toasting and buttering later. You can eat them with preserves or honey as well.

CONCLUDING REMARKS

Pikelets, as they don't have any sugar in them could also be used as a savory base for the next section of savories. We have discussed sweet teatime treats, but how about adding a savory course beforehand, to set-up the sweetness to come?

SAVORIES

INTRODUCTION

It is so very easy to produce all these savories, as part of your teatime celebration. All the London hotels that serve Afternoon Tea include some finger sandwiches, but we can do better than that! How about Mini Yorkshire puddings with cream cheese and smoked salmon? Lovely!

FINGER SANDWICHES

FINGER SANDWICHES

30 Min

FUN FACT

As you may know, the word "sandwich" comes from the Fourth Earl of Sandwich, who in about 1762 asked for his meat to be served between two slices of bread, for ease of eating, supposedly so that his gambling was not interrupted!

But what you may not know is that the First Earl was going to adopt the title Earl of Portsmouth, but changed his mind, maybe because in 1660 the fleet which he was commanding was lying off the town of Sandwich. Had he stuck with his original idea, we would all be eating portsmouths! I'll have a peanut butter and jelly portsmouth please!

Anyway, a whole new world opened up to cooks with the invention of the sandwich. I have included a few traditional finger sandwiches, but of course, you may just go for your favorite fillings. It is essential that the crusts are removed for a truly authentic experience. The joy of these sandwiches is the simplicity of great ingredients mingled together.

CUCUMBER, CREAM CHEESE AND MINT FINGER SANDWICHES

30 Min

INGREDIENTS

8 slices of buttered bread

½ cucumber sliced and then cut into matchsticks

½ bunch of fresh mint leaves, chopped

1 cup cream cheese

Freshly ground black pepper

METHOD

1. In a bowl, mix the cream cheese, mint and cucumber together.
2. Give a good twist of black pepper.
3. Lay out 4 slices of buttered bread and place a quarter of the mixture onto the 4 slices.
4. Spread well to the edges and cover with the other slices of buttered bread.
5. Carve off the crusts and cut into finger sandwiches, depending on the shape of your slices, probably into threes.

EGG AND CRESS SANDWICHES

30 Min

INGREDIENTS
8 slices of white bread - no need to butter

6 eggs

4 tablespoons mayonnaise

1 pack of cress or chopped watercress (about 1 cup) or the green part of a scallion, finely chopped

Salt and pepper

METHOD
1. Add the eggs in their shells to a saucepan of cold water and bring to the boil. It will boil a lot quicker if you have the lid on.
2. After the water begins to boil, turn down the heat to a gentle simmer for 6 minutes.
3. Cool down the eggs by running under cold water and gently remove the shells.
4. Place the naked eggs in a bowl and mash up together using a fork.
5. Add 4 tablespoons of mayonnaise, a few good twists of pepper and some salt to taste and mix well.
6. Spread the mixture over half the slices of bread right to the edges and top with the cress and another slice of bread.
7. Carve off the crusts and cut into finger sandwiches, probably into threes.

SMOKED SALMON SANDWICHES

30 Min

There are very many options with smoked salmon, but for me the simplicity of the brown bread, butter, smoked salmon, lemon and black pepper cannot be beaten. I always find other ingredients get in the way of this sublime combination.

INGREDIENTS

8 slices of buttered brown bread
4 slices of smoked salmon
Lemon juice
Black pepper

METHOD

1. Place sliced smoked salmon on half the buttered slices of bread.
2. Give a squeeze of lemon juice.
3. Give a good twist of pepper and place the other buttered slice on top.
4. Carve off the crusts and cut into three fingers.

HAM AND ENGLISH MUSTARD SANDWICHES

30 Min

FUN FACT

It was the Romans who probably first experienced mustard as a condiment. They mixed unfermented grape juice- the "must" - with ground mustard seeds to make a burning must or mustum ardens in Latin - hence "mustard." English mustard is very strong and pungent compared with French or American mustards so don't be too generous in using it!

INGREDIENTS

8 slices of buttered brown bread
4 slices of ham
English Mustard - about 2 teaspoons

METHOD

1. Place sliced ham on half the buttered slices of bread.
2. Spread the English Mustard very thinly on to the other buttered slice.
3. Marry one ham with one mustard slice.
4. Carve off the crusts and cut into three fingers.

MINI YORKSHIRE PUDDINGS

These are from Yorkshire and are traditionally served hot with roast beef for Sunday Lunch. But made smaller they serve beautifully as a small savory at teatime. If using the cream cheese toppings, serve cold or else the cheese will make a sticky mess!

MINI YORKSHIRE PUDDINGS

INGREDIENTS (MAKES 24)
3 tablespoons oil
1 ⅓ cups all-purpose flour
⅔ cup milk
4 eggs
salt, pepper

METHOD
1. Pre-heat the oven to 350° F.
2. Place a teaspoon of oil into each mold of a 24-hole mini muffin tin and put it in the oven until smoking hot.
3. Place the flour in a mixing bowl and make a well in the middle.
4. Add the eggs and milk and whisk together with a balloon whisk. Leave to one side until the oil in the muffin tin is really hot.
5. Add 2 pinches of salt and one of pepper to the batter.
6. Place about a generous tablespoon of batter into each muffin hole until you have filled up all 24 of them.
7. Bake for 28-30 minutes.
8. Remove from the oven, and leave to cool.

TOPPINGS

I think that cream cheese goes fabulously with Yorkshire puddings. It is one of those pairings that just work. I have given the quantities for 12 mini Yorkshire puddings.

SMOKED SALMON AND CREAM CHEESE

INGREDIENTS
3 slices of smoked salmon cut into quarters
1 cup cream cheese
Lemon juice to spritz
Black pepper

METHOD
1. Place a teaspoon or so of cream cheese in the middle of the Yorkshire.

2. Curl up the smoked salmon and push it gently into the cream cheese.

3. When you have made all 12, line them up for a lemon spritz and a good twisting of black pepper. Serve and enjoy!

BEEF AND HORSERADISH SAUCE

FUN FACT
Ancient Greeks used horseradish as a back rub and as an aphrodisiac. It is very strong, so a little goes a long way.

INGREDIENTS
3 slices of thinly cut roast beef cut into quarters.
3 teaspoons of horseradish sauce.
Parsley for garnish.

METHOD
1. Curl up the beef and push it gently into the Yorkshire.

2. Add a small blob of horseradish.

3. Garnish with some parsley.

CUCUMBER, MINT AND CREAM CHEESE

INGREDIENTS
½ cucumber sliced and then cut into matchsticks.
½ bunch of fresh mint leaves, chopped (save some for the garnish)
1 cup cream cheese

METHOD

1. In a bowl, mix the cream cheese, mint and cucumber together.

2. Add a teaspoon or so into the middle of your Yorkshire puddings.

3. Garnish with a little chopped mint.

CONCLUDING REMARKS

So lots of wonderful ideas for savory teatime treats. Of course, any of the recipes stand alone as a teatime treat, but what if you want to celebrate a special occasion, a birthday, anniversary, baby shower, or just to treat a special friend. How about putting together a traditional English Afternoon Tea with all the trimmings?

How about if each guest were to make one recipe and then combine them all for the celebration, perhaps one of the 30 Minutes from Measure to Munch recipes? You would have a wonderful celebration with only 30 minutes of work each!

The following section will show you how to combine the recipes to produce a spectacular English Afternoon Tea that everyone will remember and love!

PUTTING IT ALL TOGETHER

AN ENGLISH AFTERNOON TEA CELEBRATION

INTRODUCTION

Traditionally, English Afternoon Tea is presented on a 3-tier cake stand. The lowest tier will contain your savory items, the middle tier has the scones, preserves and cream and the top tier has your sweet and delicious teatime treats.

LOWEST TIER - SAVORIES

Select two or three Finger Sandwiches or a Finger Sandwich and a mini Yorkshire pudding. For example, egg and cress presented on white bread, and Smoked Salmon on brown. If you stand them cut-side up alternating the sandwiches, it gives a very pleasing presentation. Perhaps the Yorkshire puddings topped with cucumber, cream cheese and mint would go well also.

MIDDLE TIER - SCONES

Select one of the scones, probably the most traditional would be a fruited scone, with strawberry preserves and cream. If you have an Afternoon

Tea in England, you will be presented with the scones and two pots, one for the preserves, and one for the cream, for you to assemble the scone yourself. You may wish to do this for your guests, or assemble the scones for them.

TOP TIER - TEATIME TREATS

This is where I have devoted most of this book so you have a wonderful selection of treats to choose from! I would select something with chocolate, some type of cake and a biscuit or something from the Exotic Teatime Treats section, for example, chocolate Tiffin, Lavender Shortbread and a slice of Medieval Honey Cake. To avoid any disagreements, do make sure that there is enough for everyone to have one of each of the treats! They may not all fit on the plate, but refills are permitted!

CONCLUDING REMARKS

I hope that you will find inspiration to create something wonderful in the kitchen, to turn a catch-up into an occasion, to turn an achievement into a celebration, to bring back the wonderful homely fragrance of something that you have made as a gift for someone you care about. If this book has helped you a little to seize life's delights and transform them into moments then I am satisfied.

What are you waiting for - in 30 minutes from measure to munch you could be eating one of these delicious treats!

CONVERSIONS

For all my European friends, I would love you to use these recipes. I would recommend getting some cup measurers, (cheaply available from the internet) but for your ease, I have included here two conversion tables for butter and for oven temperatures, which need converting for those outside the USA.

BUTTER CONVERSIONS

1/4 cup is 57 grams   1/3 cup is 76 grams
1/2 cup is 113 grams   1 cup is 227 grams

OVEN TEMPERATURES

°F	°C	Fan	Gas
300	150	130	2
325	170	150	3
350	180	160	4
375	190	170	5
400	200	180	6
425	220	200	7
450	230	210	8

ACKNOWLEDGMENTS

I would love to thank my wonderful family for their unending encouragement. Special thanks to my husband, Simon, who believed in me from the start and always encouraged me to explore cooking. Thanks to my daughter, Poppy, who was happy to pretend to be an inexperienced cook with her friends to test out some recipes. My son, Monty, has always been very enthusiastic and helpful with his creative comments, my thanks. Thank you to Barty, my youngest son, for being such a delight and ever willing to scrape the remainders of the mix once we were done!

To my mother, Angela, who has inspired me always with her amazing creative cooking and her ability to search for easy shortcuts to delicious food. Thank you to my father for encouraging me in my Food and Nutrition course and for eating nut cutlets for a whole week without complaining!

My sisters, Louise and Emma, have always been amazing and so kind to me. Thank you all for coming with me on this journey; I am so blessed to have such an amazing family!

Thank you to my Mother-in-law, Molly, for being such an encourager and for your enthusiasm for my creations. Thanks to my late father-in-law, Norman, who particularly loved the Fruit Cake in this book.

For the help from my brilliant editor, William Gaskill, who has set this cookbook on the road to publishing, my wonderful recipe-tester Alicia Clemens and to the amazing Ida Fia Sveningsson for creating the visuals and designing the layout for this — I would be lost without you all!

Thank you to God, the Creator of All and the Great Alchemist for the gift of life.

ABOUT THE AUTHOR

Sandra Hawkins is qualified in many disciplines. She is a chemist, banker, lawyer, teacher, apologist, author, wife, mother of three and a qualified Indian head massage therapist! However, she also has a real passion for food and is an exceptional chef.

Combining her love for mixing things up in a chemistry lab with her natural gift as a supertaster, Sandra has always loved to experiment with cooking.

From her very first Food and Nutrition lessons at an English school (Guildford High) to exploring Indian and African cuisine while traveling and living overseas, Sandra is particularly passionate about using cooking to bring people together and to seize life's delights and transform them into moments.

This book reflects her passion for food and her unique ability to simplify complex recipes, so people can easily enjoy traditional English teatime treats at home for the first time.

Sandra is married to songwriter/producer/author, Simon Hawkins and has three beautiful children, Poppy, Monty and Barty . They live in a quiet village on a beach on the south coast of England, in West Sussex.

THANK YOU FOR BUYING THIS BOOK!

I really appreciate all of your feedback, and I love hearing what you have to say. I also need your input to make the next version better. Please leave me a helpful REVIEW on Amazon!
Thank you so much!

Sandra

www.ingramcontent.com/pod-product-compliance
Lightning Source LLC
Chambersburg PA
CBHW061928290426
44113CB00024B/2842

9780995762312